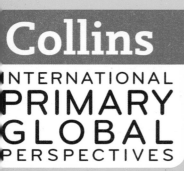

Collins

INTERNATIONAL
PRIMARY
GLOBAL
PERSPECTIVES

Student's Book 1

Published by Collins

An imprint of HarperCollins*Publishers*
The News Building, 1 London Bridge Street, London,
SE1 9GF, UK

HarperCollins*Publishers*
Macken House, 39/40 Mayor Street Upper, Dublin 1 D01 C9W8

Browse the complete Collins catalogue at
collins.co.uk

© HarperCollins*Publishers* Limited 2023

10 9 8 7 6 5 4 3 2 1

ISBN 978-0-00-854952-7

Series editor: Nick Coates
Author: Daphne Paizee
Publisher: Elaine Higgleton
Product developer: Roisin Leahy
Development editor: Lucy Cooper
Copyeditor: Catherine Dakin
Proofreader: Gudrun Kaiser
Illustrations: Jouve India Ltd.
Contributor: Lucy Norris
Cover designer: Gordon MacGilp
Typesetter: David Jimenez, Ken Vail Graphic Design
Production controller: Lyndsey Rogers
Printed in Italy by Grafica Veneta S.p.a.

We are grateful to MInal Mistry for providing feedback on the Student's Book as it was developed.

Contents

How to use this book

Use this book in your lessons, to learn about a range of global topics!

The skills box shows you the main and subsidiary skills that you will learn and practise in this lesson.

> ✓ **Main**
> ✓ Subsidiary

📖 An activity that involves reading

🎧 An activity that involves listening

👥 An activity that involves working in a pair

👥 An activity that involves working in a group

Talking point
- You will look back on what you have learned in the lesson, and talk about things that went well with your classmates.

Before you go
- Think about how you will use your new skills!

You will see some words that are <u>underlined</u> in this book. The glossary on page 81 will tell you the meaning of these words.

Unit 1 Family and friends

What do you know?
- Who is in your family?
- How are family members related?
- Where do you live?
- Who are your friends?
- What work do your family members do?

In this unit, you will:
- Talk about your family and friends
- Make a <u>collage</u> with pictures and <u>diagrams</u>.

1.1 Who is in your family?

1 💬 Sing a song with your teacher.

2 👂 Listen to your teacher and answer the questions.

3 💬 **Talk about your family.**

What do you call your mother?

I call her *Mama.*

4 👥 **Play a game:**
Who is this?

5 ✏️💬 **Draw a picture of your family on your worksheet. Answer questions about your family.**

Talking point

- What have you learned about different families?

Before you go

- Who else is in your family?
- What are their names?

1.2 Who is in the family?

1 💬 👂 **Listen to your teacher read a story. Talk about the story you hear.**

2 💬 **Look at the pictures. What is this story about?**

Siba's family

My name is Siba.
This is my family.

This is Ma.

This is Baba.
He is my grandfather.

Alex and Ajay are my brothers.

This is Aunty Anna.
She is my mother's sister.

My cousin Dora lives with us.

3 📖 **Read the story and answer the questions.**

a **Who** is the person telling the story?
b **What** does Siba call her mother?
c **What** does Siba call her grandfather?
d **How many** brothers does Siba have?
e **Who** is Anna?
f **Where** does Dora live?

> **Key terms**
> **Who**, **What**, **Where** and **How many** are words that ask questions.

4 📖 👂 **Match the pictures to the questions on your worksheet.**

5 👥 **Work in groups of seven. Make up a story about Siba's family.**

Who is that?

That is Dora!

Talking point

- What have you learned about different families?

Before you go

- Who else is in your family?
- Do you have family in different places?

1.3 Are they related?

✓ Analysis
✓ Communication

1 💬 👂 Listen and talk about diagrams.

2 💬 What does this family tree diagram show us?

Siba's family tree

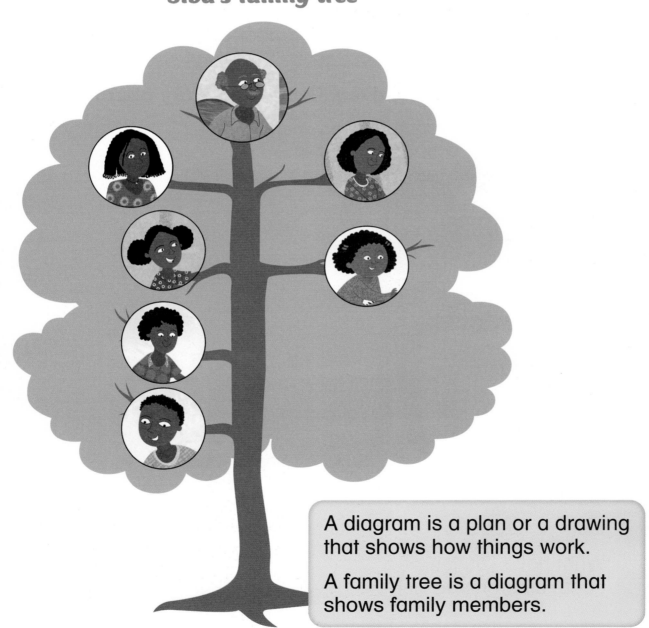

A diagram is a plan or a drawing that shows how things work.

A family tree is a diagram that shows family members.

3 📖 **Look at the diagram and answer the questions.**

a Who is the oldest person in the family?
Where is he on the tree?

b Who is Ma and Aunty Anna's father?

c Who is the youngest in the family?
Where is she on the tree?

d Where are Siba's brothers on the tree?

e Who are cousins in this family?

4 👥 **Ask and answer.**

Who is Aunty Anna's sister?

Why are Alex and Ajay here?

Talking point

• Do you understand how the family tree diagram works?

Before you go

• Do you have an aunt? Is she the sister of your mother or father?

• How are people in your family related?

1.4 Can you draw a family tree diagram?

1 👥 Work in groups.
Make a family tree.

2 💬 Look at this story. What is the story about? Who are the family in the story?

The Lee family

This is the Lee family.

They have one child.
His name is Hu.

Grandmother Lao Lao is mother's mother.

Yeye is father's father.

8

Uncle Min is mother's brother.   Mei is Uncle Min's daughter.

3 📖 **Read the story and answer the questions.**

a **How many** people are in this family?

b **What** is the family name?

c **Who** is Hu?

d **Who** is Mei?

e **What** is the name of the grandfather?

4 👥 **Use your worksheets to make a family tree diagram of the Lee family.**

5 💬 **Talk about your Lee family tree diagram.**

Talking point

- What did your partner do to help you make a tree diagram?

Before you go

- Do the diagrams help you to understand the story you read? How?

1.5 Who are our friends?

1 💬 👂 **What do you know about friends? Listen to your teacher and talk about what you hear.**

2 💬 **Look at the pictures of friends. What are they doing together? How are they helping each other?**

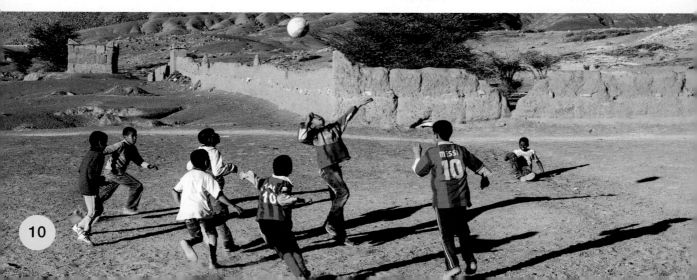

3 👥 **Act out something that a friend does.**

4 👥 **What do friends do? Complete a diagram about friends on your worksheet.**

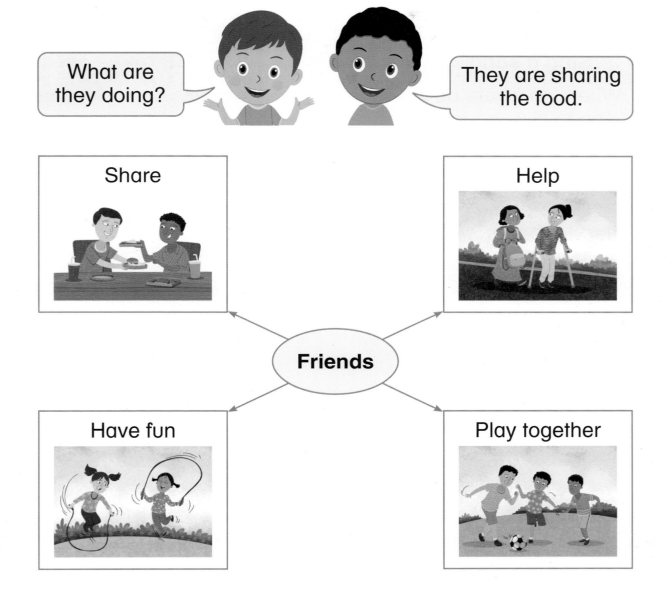

1.6 What do people in your family do?

1 💬 **Sing a song.**

Where oh where do we go to play,
   go to play, go to play?
Where oh where do we go to play?
The park with the yellow slide, I say!

2 👥 **Look at the pictures. What is the story about? Read the story.**

Out and about

It is time to go.

Aunty drives the bus.

My brother goes to school.

This teacher goes to school.

A friend works in an office.

My mother is a nurse at a hospital.

The bus stops.
They get off the bus.

They work in the city.

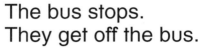
3 Discuss the story.

How do they get to work and school?

Who works in a city?

4 **a** **Listen to a talk.**

What is the speaker's name?
What is their job?

b Ask the speaker some questions.

Where do you work?

5 **Write questions on your worksheet. Then talk about the jobs that family members do.**

Talking point

- What did you enjoy about this lesson?

Before you go

Ask questions about people in your community:

- What do _____ do?
- Why is a _____ important?

Unit 1 Final task: Make a collage

What can you tell us about family and friends?

What?	Make a collage about family and friends.
	Present your collage to the class.
	Use the collage to answer questions.
How?	Work in groups.

How can you be successful in this task? Listen to your teacher.

Success means ...
We worked together to make the collage.
We used pictures and diagrams in the collage.
We answered questions about the collage.

1 Talk about this collage.

What can you see?

14

2 👥 **Discuss the collage you will make.**

What do you need?

Checklist

Do you have these?
- ✓ Pictures of family
- ✓ Pictures of friends
- ✓ Pictures about community
- ✓ Family tree diagrams

3 👥 **Work in groups. Make a collage.**

Tips

- Make your collage big.
- Use colours.
- Use leaves, sticks, string and pieces of material.

You would like people to look at the collage and ask questions.

4 👥 **Show your collage to the class.**
Answer questions about your collage.

What does this diagram show?

Who is this?

Where is the person?

Does the person work?

Where does the person live?

What do friends do?

Tips

Listen carefully to the questions.
- What is the question about? (A person? A place?)
- Give short clear answers.

Reflection: How successful were our collages?

Final task checklist			
Did you work together to make the collage?	☺	😐	☹
Did you use pictures and diagrams?	☺	😐	☹
Did you answer questions about the collage?	☺	😐	☹

What did someone in your group do to help you?

a Did they help you to answer a question?

b Did they explain a diagram?

c Did they show you a picture?

d Did they help you to plan the collage?

Before you go

- What did you learn about families and friends in this unit?
- What did you learn about working in a group?

Unit 2 Am I healthy?

What do you know?
- What can we do to be healthy?
- Why do we get toothache?
- Is all our food healthy?
- What foods do we grow in our area?
- Are all plants safe to eat?

In this unit, you will:
- Talk about what you can do to be healthy
- Make a book to explain your ideas about how to be healthy.

2.1 How can we be healthy?

1 💬 **Talk about being healthy.**

2 👥 **Talk about the pictures.**

a Which pictures show children doing healthy things?

b What keeps us healthy?

3 👥 **Make a page for a book about what you can do to be healthy.**

Talking point

- What have you learned in this lesson?

Before you go

- Sing a song about what you do to be healthy.

2.2 Why do we get toothache?

✓ Research
✓ Evaluation

1 💬 **Why do we brush our teeth?**

2 💬 **How can we find out what happens to our teeth?**

a Put one egg into each glass. Be careful!

b What do you think will happen? Record your <u>predictions</u> on the worksheet.

i — Cola

ii — Juice

iii — Vinegar

iv — Water

c Take out the eggs. What happened to the eggs? Record what you see on your worksheet.

d You are going to brush the eggs from liquids **i** and **ii** with toothpaste and a brush. What do you think will happen? Record what you predict on your worksheet.

3 So, what do you think now? Should we brush our teeth? What might happen if we don't?

4 Make another page for your book. Show what you think about keeping your teeth healthy.

Talking point

- What did you enjoy about the <u>investigation</u>?

Before you go

- What other tips can you give your friends about healthy teeth?

2.3 Is your food healthy?

1 🗨 🔊 **What do you know about healthy foods?**

2 🗨 **What is this story about?**

What do you think?

There are lots. What can we do with them?

What do *you* think?

3  **Read the story. Ask and answer questions.**

Do carrots from the garden taste better than carrots from the shop?

How can we make food safe to eat?

Useful language

What do you think?
I think that …

4 **Make a page about healthy food for your book.**

Talking point

• Can you give an opinion about healthy food?

Before you go

• How can you grow your own food?

2.4 Which senses do you use?

1 💬 What are the five <u>senses</u> that we use?

touch smell taste hearing sight

2 ✏️ 💬 Ask your friends which two senses they use the most. Record their answers on your worksheet.

3 👥 What is it? Smell and taste the foods.

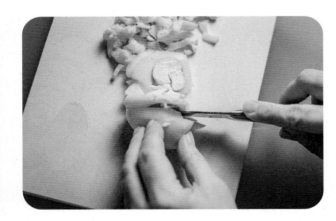

4 💬 **Talk about the foods you tasted.**

5 👥 **Make a page for your book about a food that you tasted.**

Talking point

- What did you enjoy in this lesson?

Before you go

- Which tastes do you enjoy the most?

2.5 Are all plants good to eat?

1 👥 **What plants do we eat?**

What plant does it come from?

What part of the plant is it?

2 💬 **Are all plants safe to eat? How can you find out?**

3 📖 💬 **Do you know these plants? Find out more from the diagram. Use the pictures to help you to answer the questions.**

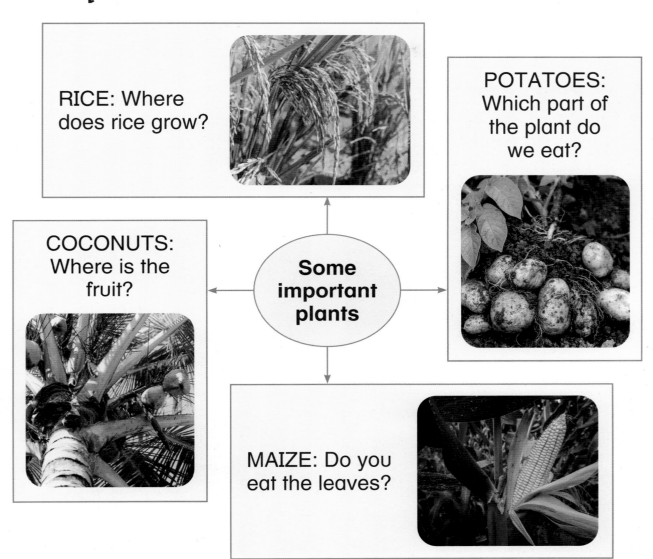

RICE: Where does rice grow?

POTATOES: Which part of the plant do we eat?

COCONUTS: Where is the fruit?

Some important plants

MAIZE: Do you eat the leaves?

4 👥 **Make a page for your book about plants that you eat.**

Talking point
- What did you share about the foods in the diagram?

Before you go
- What other plants do you eat?

2.6 What do you know about local foods?

Where will you look for food?

1 💬 **Prepare for your food hunt.**

How do you know if it is healthy or safe to eat?

How do you know if the food is local?

2 👥 **Find local foods in your area.**

3 👥 **What foods did you find on the trip? Make a page for your book about the food hunt.**

Talking point

- How did your partner help you on the trip?

Before you go

- Is it good to buy and use local foods?

Unit 2 Final task: Make a book about being healthy

How can we be healthy?

What?	Complete your book about how to be healthy. Put the pages together and make a cover.
	Present your book to your group.
	Use the book to explain your ideas to the group.
How?	Work in pairs.

How can you be successful in this task? Listen to your teacher.

Success means …
We worked together to make a book about how to be healthy.
We stated our opinions about how to be healthy.
We asked and answered questions about how to be healthy.

1 Understand the task.

Discuss the book that you are making.
- How many pages have you made already?
- Do you want to make any more pages?
- How will you put the pages together to make your book?
- Will the book have a cover with a name?

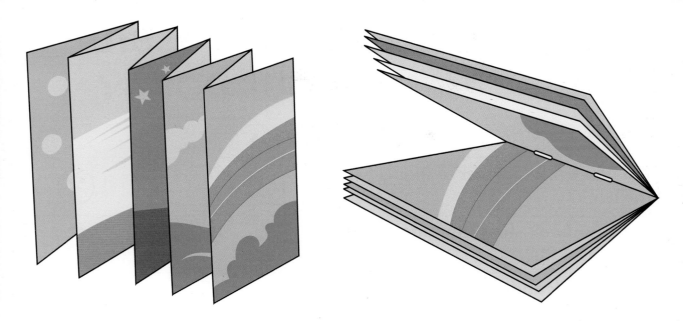

You can make different types of books.

2 👥 **Work in pairs. Make your book.**

Are these in your book?
✓ Ideas about keeping your body clean.
✓ Ideas about healthy food.
✓ Ideas about what else you can do to be healthy.

3 👥 **Explain your ideas about how to be healthy.**

- Use pages from your book to explain what you mean.
- Remember to give your opinion.

Tips

Use words like this:
- I/We think that …
- I/We don't think that …

Reflection: How successful was our book?

Final task checklist			
Did you work together to make the book?	😊	😐	☹️
Did your book show your ideas about being healthy?	😊	😐	☹️
Did you ask and answer questions about the book?	😊	😐	☹️

What did you learn about being healthy?

a What kind of food is important?

b What else can you do to be healthy?

c Are all plants safe to eat?

Before you go

- What else would you like to learn about keeping healthy?
- What could we do to learn about this?

Unit 3 Water, water everywhere

What do you know?
- Where can we find water?
- What do we use water for at home?
- Why is water important?
- What can you do in water?
- Does it float?
- How can we share water?

In this unit, you will:
- Talk about how we use water and why it is important
- Make a poster to show a water <u>problem</u> and a <u>solution</u> to the problem.

3.1 Where can we find water?

1 💬 **Discuss the photographs.**

2 👥 **Complete the picture on your worksheet.**

3 👂 **Listen to *Incy Wincy Spider*. What is it about?**

> Incy Wincy Spider went up the waterspout
> Down came the rain and washed the spider out
> Out came the sun and dried up all the rain
> So, Incy Wincy Spider went up the spout again

4 💬 👥 **What can the spider do?**

Talking point

- What did you enjoy in this lesson?

Before you go

- How do you keep dry when it rains?

3.2 What do we use water for at home?

1 👥 Act out how you use water at home.

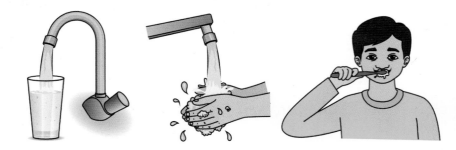

2 💬 Make a diagram about using water at home.

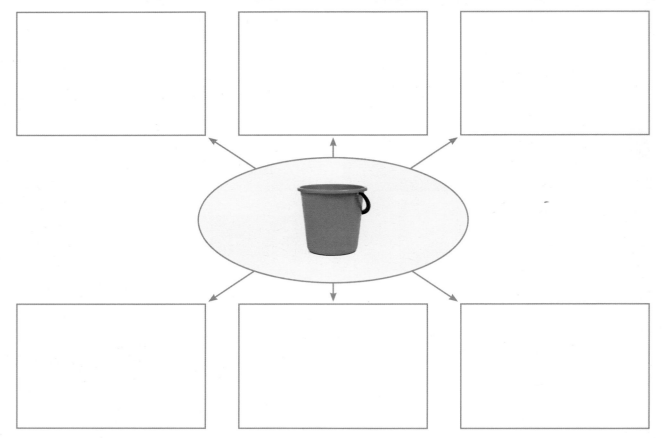

3 Use your worksheet to make a diagram about how you use water at home.

4 What does this picture show? What is happening in the photos? Discuss what you do with water in your home.

Talking point

- What did you learn?

Before you go

- Can you sing a song about water?

3.3 Why is water important?

1 💬 **Discuss the pictures.**

2 💬 **What happens when there is no water?**

3 ✏️ **Draw a picture showing what happens when there is no water.**

4 💬 **Answer questions about your picture.**

Talking point

- What did you learn about how we use water?

Before you go

- Why is water important where you live?

3.4 What can you do in water?

1 💬 What can you see in the pictures?

2 💬 **Play a game.**

Questions

What questions can you ask?

Where do you do this?

When do you do this?

What do you use?

How do you do this?

3 ✏️ **On your worksheet, draw a picture of things you can do in water.**

4 💬 **Answer questions about your picture.**

Talking point

• What did you enjoy in this lesson?

Before you go

• What water sports do you want to try?

3.5 Does it float?

1  **Will they float or sink in water?**
Record what you see on your worksheet.

2 **Listen to a story.**
What did the crow
want to do? What was
the problem?

3 👥 **What can the crow do? Choose a solution on your worksheet and colour it in.**

4 👥 **Try the crow's solution. Does it work?**

Talking point

- Can you name some things that sink in water?

Before you go

- How can you make something float?

3.6 How can we share water?

1 💬 **Look at the pictures.**

- Where are the animals?
- Why are they near water?

2 📖 **Read the story. What did Hare do?**

Hare and the waterhole

Giraffe, elephant, antelope, hare and lion lived in the same place.

They shared water and food.

One year there was a drought.

The animals dug a waterhole.

Hare drank all the water
at night.

'What can we do?'
said King Giraffe.

3 What can the animals do? Discuss your ideas and
draw a solution on your worksheet.

4 Act out a story to show how to share water.

Talking point

- How did you help to act
  out the story? Did you
  support your group?

Before you go

- How can we
  share water?

Unit 3 Final task: Make a poster!

What can we do?

What?	Make a poster about how to look after water.
	Present your poster to your class.
How?	Work in groups.

🔊 **How can you be successful in this task? Listen to your teacher.**

Success means …
We discussed water problems.
We suggested solutions to water problems.
We worked together to make a poster about water problems and solutions.

1 💬 👥 **Look at the pictures. What are the problems?**

2 👥 **Work in groups. Choose solutions on the worksheet.**

3 👥 **Choose a problem about water. Make a poster.**

Did you discuss the problems and solutions?

Does your poster show a problem and a solution?

4 💬 **Talk about your poster.**

Tips

What is your opinion about the problem you have chosen?

- Is it a big problem or a small problem?
- Can we do something about it?

Reflection: How successful were our posters?

Final task checklist			
Did you identify a water problem?	🙂	😐	🙁
Did you discuss and find a solution to show on your poster?	🙂	😐	🙁
Did you ask and answer questions about your poster?	🙂	😐	🙁

What did you enjoy about this task?

a What did you enjoy about the discussions?

b What did you enjoy about making a poster?

Before you go

- What can you do to save water?
- What can you do to share water?

Unit (4) What a waste!

What do you know?
- What is it made of?
- What <u>waste</u> is there at school?
- What can we learn from animals about recycling?
- Let's play games!
- What will happen to it?
- How can we <u>reuse</u> things?

In this unit, you will:
- Talk about reusing materials that we don't want any more
- Make an object out of <u>junk</u>
- Make up a story about the object you made.

4.1 What is it made of?

1 💬 **Discuss the diagrams.**

A

B

C

D

plastic

wood

metal

paper

DAILY NEWS

2 👥 **Sort the objects into groups.**

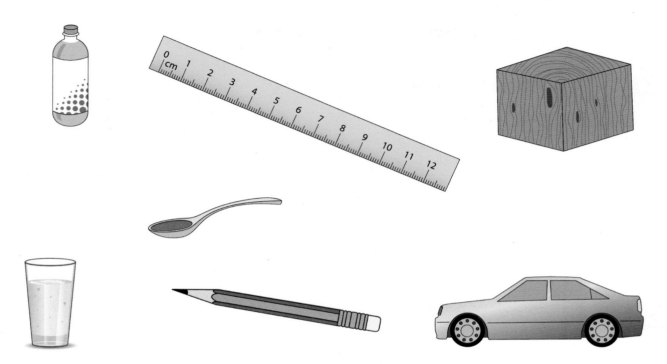

3 ✏️ **Record the information on your worksheet.**

4 💬 **Talk about a problem. What do you do with something you don't want any more?**

What happens to plastic that has already been used?

Can we throw it away? Where?

Will it make a mess?

Talking point

- What did you learn from your diagrams?

Before you go

- Do you use plastic bottles?

4.2 What waste is there at school?

1 💬 **Talk about the diagram.**

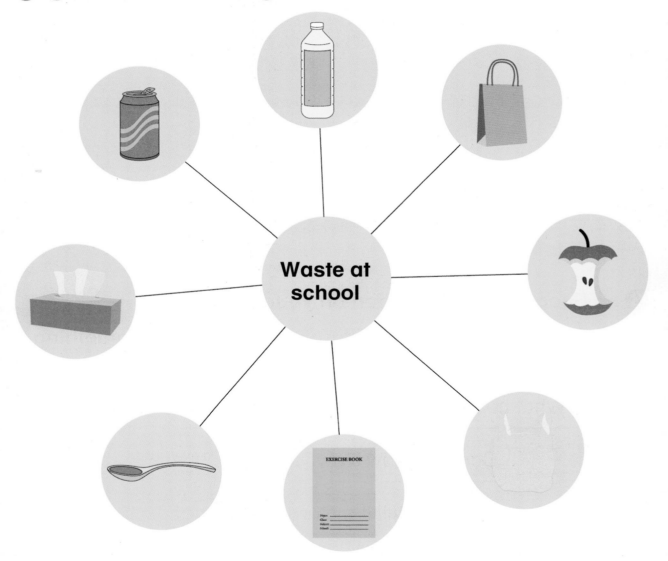

Waste at school

2 💬 👥 **Start an investigation about waste at your school. Work in groups and discuss what questions you will ask to start your investigation.**

Where ...?   What ...?

3 👥 **Do your investigation. What will each of you do?**

4 💬 **Talk about your investigation. Talk about what your group found out.**

> We found out that …

> We helped each other to …

> One problem is …

Talking point

- What did you learn about working in a group?

Before you go

- What else would you like to know about waste at your school?
- What would you like to do?

4.3 What can we learn from animals?

1 💬 Animals use things more than once. What do you think these crabs reuse?

2 👥 Look at the nests in the photographs. What do the birds reuse?

3 👥 **What can we reuse to make something?**

4 ✏️ **Record your ideas on your worksheet.**

5 💬 **Talk about what you found out.**

Talking point

- What did you enjoy in these activities?

Before you go

- What would you use to make a nest or a web?

4.4 Let's play games!

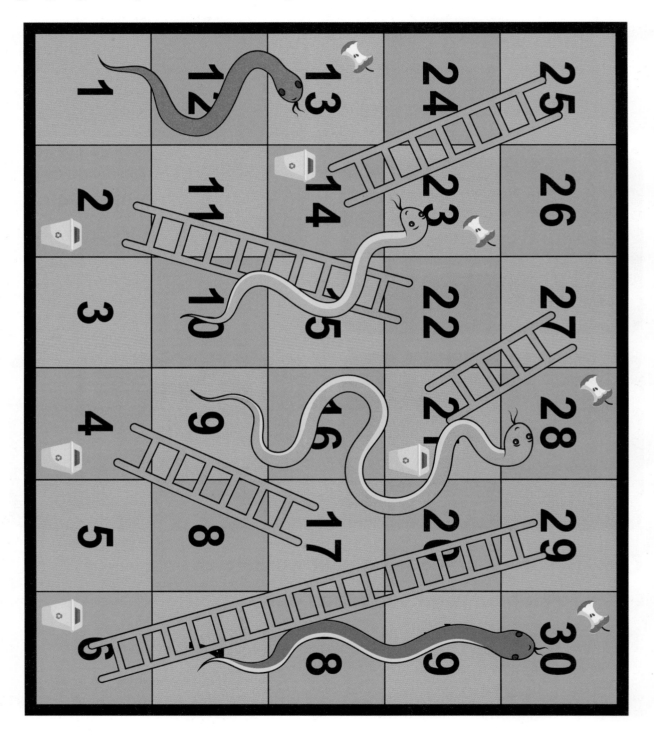

✓ Collaboration
✓ Communication

1 💬 👥 **Do you know this game?**

2 🗪 👥 **Teach your partner how to play a game.**

What do you need? | You need …

What do you do? | First you … Then you …

Who wins? | The winner is the one who …

A <u>recycle</u> relay

Water bottle bowling

3 👥 **Prepare the materials you need to play a game.**

4 👥 **Play one of the games in groups.**

Talking point
- What did you enjoy in these activites?

Before you go
- What other games can you explain to your friends?

4.5 What will happen to it?

1 💬 **Talk about the picture.**

2 📖 **Do you know what 'junk' is? Read the story.**

Not junk!

This is Zap. Zap picks up junk.

The box is not junk.

Zap has a shell. Is it junk?

The shell is not junk.

Is this a laptop? Is this a ship?

Yes. The box is not junk.

3 💬 **Discuss the questions.**

a What is the title of the story?

b What does Zap do?

c Is the box junk?

d What do they make with the box?

e What can you make with a box?

f What happens if you don't reuse boxes?

4 👥 **Make up a story about something that was thrown away but was then reused.**

5 👥 **Tell your story to the class, to another pair or group. Or, act it out.**

Talking point

- What did you learn from the story?
- Why do people collect junk?

Before you go

- What can you do with plastic bottles and containers?
- What other junk can you use again?

59

4.6 How can we reuse things?

1 💬 **What is it made of? Talk about the photographs.**

2 Make something new.

Checklist

✓ What can you make?
✓ What can you use?
✓ Is it hard or soft?
✓ Can you bend it?
✓ Can you glue it?
✓ How long will it take?

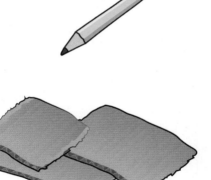

3 Record what you made on your worksheet.

4 Improve your objects.

Talking point

• What did you learn from this activity?
• Was it easy to share things?

Before you go

• What else could you have made?

Unit 4 Final task: Write a story about an object made from reused materials

✓ **Collaboration**
✓ Research
✓ Reflection

How can we reuse this?

What?	Make up a story about an object made from reused materials.
	Tell your story to the class, or act it out.
How?	Work in groups.

🔊 **How can you be successful in this task? Listen to your teacher.**

Success means ...
We made up a story about the object we made.
We worked together to tell or act out the story.

① 👥 **Understand the task.**

Checklist

Look at the object you made.
✓ Is it complete?
✓ Are you happy with it?
✓ What can you add to it?
✓ How can you make it better?

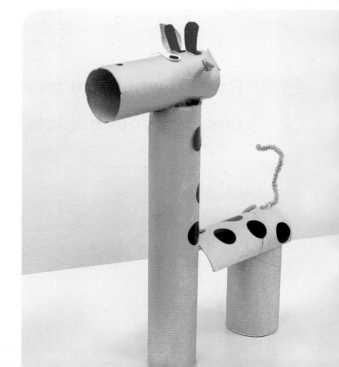

2 🎧 **Listen to the story about one of the objects in the pictures.**

3 👥 **Make up a story about your object.**

Where does it come from?

What was it used for before?

Who owned it?

What does it do now?

4 👥 **Tell or act out the story for the class.**

Checklist

We work together to:
✓ make up a story
✓ tell or act out the story.

Reflection: How successful was our object and our story?

Final task checklist			
Did you make up a good story?	☺	😐	☹
Did you all make suggestions?	☺	😐	☹
Did you have enough time to improve the stories?	☺	😐	☹

How successful were stories?

a What questions did you ask each other when you made up your stories?

b Did you all take part?

c Did the class ask questions about them?

d What could you have done better?

What did you do to help your group?

a What suggestions did you make?

b What did you do to help make up and share a story?

Before you go

- What else can you use to make fun objects?

Unit 5 Getting the message

What do you know?
- How do we <u>communicate</u> with each other?
- What can you hear?
- Are you a good listener?
- Does music talk to us?
- How can we make different sounds?
- What is the message?

In this unit, you will:
- Talk about how we communicate with other people
- Find out about sign language and use it to communicate a short message.

5.1 How do we communicate with each other?

1 💬 Look at the faces. What do they tell us?

2 👥 Can you guess how I feel?

3 💬 How do we send messages?

What is this used for?

How does it work?

What do you need to use it?

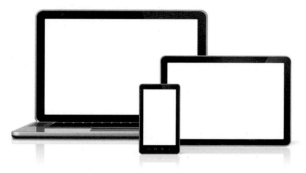

4 ✏️ Listen and draw faces on your worksheet.

Talking point
- What did you enjoy in this lesson?

Before you go
- How else can you communicate with others?

5.2 What can you hear?

1 💬 **Talk about the pictures.**

What sounds do you hear?

What makes the sounds?

How do the sounds make you feel?

2 💬 **Look at this <u>pictogram</u>. It has pictures and numbers about sounds in a park. Talk about it with your teacher.**

Sounds	How many?	Total
birds		4
cars		2
talking		5
music		8

3 👥 **Listen to sounds and record what you hear on your worksheet.**

4 ✏️ **Make a pictogram that shows the sounds you heard.**

Talking point

- What did you learn from the pictograms?

Before you go

Look at the pictures on the right.

- What are they?
- How can you use these to give messages?
- When would you use them?

5.3 Are you a good listener?

1 💬 **Are you a good listener? Play a game to find out.**

2 💬 **What do we do when we listen?**

Please give the book to Maya.

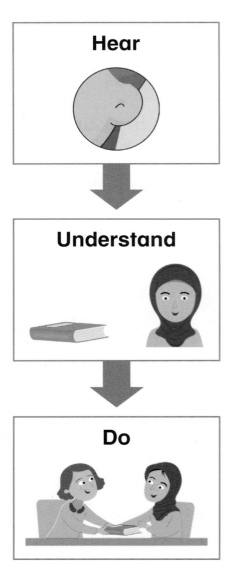

Hear

Understand

Do

3 💬 👥 **How can we listen well?**

Think about these questions:

Do you talk when you listen?

Do you keep still?

What do you do if you don't understand what you hear?

What else do you do?

4 👂 👥 **Listen and draw.**

Talking point

- What did you do to listen well?

Before you go

- Play another listening game.

5.4 Does music talk to us?

1 💬 How does music 'talk' to you?

2 💬 Talk about the <u>musical instruments</u> in the pictures.

Can you describe the sounds they make?

What are they made of?

How do you play them?

Why do we play them?

What do you do when you hear this music?

3 👥 **Ask questions and find out more about the instruments.**

Follow these steps:

1 Choose an instrument. Find a picture if you can.

2 Think of four questions you want to ask and write them on your worksheet.

3 Decide how to answer the questions.

4 Write the answers on the worksheet.

4 💬 👥 **What did you find out? Tell your group.**

Talking point

- Did you ask good questions about your instrument?
- Can you think of one better question?

Before you go

- What kind of music do you like to play? Why?

5.5 How can we make different sounds?

1 💬 **What sounds can you make?**

2 💬 **Ask and answer questions about the bucket drums.**

> What are the instruments made of?

> Could they make different sounds? How?

3 💬 **Set up an investigation to find out if objects can make different sounds.**

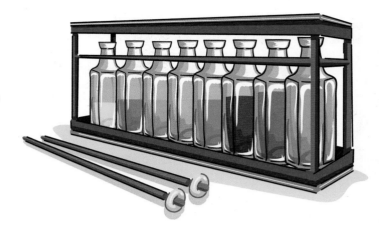

Make a water xylophone.

> **What you need**

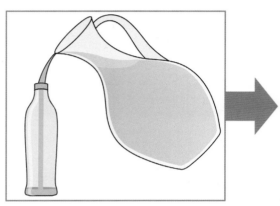

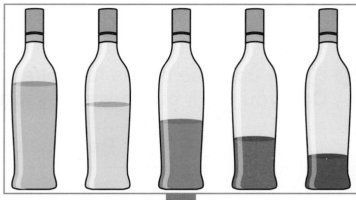

4 💬 **Investigate the sounds made by the different bottles.**

- What did you find out?
- Did the bottles make the same sounds? Why or why not?

Answer the questions on your worksheet.

> **Talking point**
>
> - What did you enjoy about this lesson?

> **Before you go**
> - Can you play a tune on one of the instruments you made?

5.6 What is the message?

1 💬 👥 **What do these signs mean?**

2 👥 **We can use codes to make messages. Can you work out these messages?**

> Read the code first.

1	9	15	13	8	16	25	20
a	I	o	m	h	p	y	t

a 9   1   13   8   1   16   16   25

b 9   1   13   8   15   20

3 👥 **We can also use letters of the alphabet to write a code. Work out the messages on your worksheet.**

4 👥 **Can you send a message with your body? What do you think they are saying with their bodies?**

5 👥 **Take turns to act out a message with your body for your group.**

Talking point

- What did you enjoy about this activity?

Before you go

- How do codes help us to communicate?

Unit 5 Final task: Give a short message in sign language

What?	Find out about another way of communicating.
How?	Work in pairs.

👂 **How can you be successful in this task? Listen to your teacher.**

Success means ...
We find out more about sign language.
We help each other to use some sign language.
We use sign language to give a simple message.

1 💬 👥 **Talk about the pictures.**

How is the boy communicating?
- Do you understand what he is saying?
- Can you communicate like this?

Eat

Drink

More

Please

Thank you

Sorry

2 👥 **Talk about sign language.**

Look at the photographs.

- What do you think the girls are saying?
- Is sign language useful?

Discuss this with your group.

3 👥 **a** **Look at the alphabet of sign language.**

- Which letters are in your name?
- Try to sign these letters.

b Sign your name to your group.

A   B   C   D   E   F   G

H   I   J   K   L   M   N

O   P   Q   R   S   T   U

V   W   X   Y   Z

4 👥 **Can you spell out one of the messages in sign language?**

- What do you need to do?

Hello!	This is good.
My name is …	He is my friend.
I am sorry.	She is tall.

5 👥 **Sign your message to the class. Answer questions about your message.**

Tip

Make the message short and clear.

Reflection: How successful was your communication?

a Discuss the task with your group.

Final task checklist			
Did you agree on which message to send?	🙂	😐	🙁
Did you agree on how to sign the message?	🙂	😐	🙁
Did you help each other?	🙂	😐	🙁
Did the class understand your message?	🙂	😐	🙁
Why is sign language useful?	🙂	😐	🙁

b Complete the final worksheet.

Before you go

- What did you enjoy about the task?
- What did you find difficult?
- Will you use sign language?

Glossary

collage: A collage is a picture that you make by sticking pieces of paper or cloth on a surface. 1

communicate: If you communicate with someone, you share information with other people, for example, by speaking, writing or using equipment. 65

diagram: A diagram is a simple drawing of the lines used, for example, to explain how a machine works. 1

investigation: If you carry out an investigation, you try to find out how something happened. 21

junk: Junk is old and useless things that you do not want or need. 69

musical instrument: A musical instrument is an object such as a piano, guitar or violin, which you play to produce music. 72

pictogram: A pictogram is a simple drawing that represents something. 49

prediction: If you make a prediction about something, you say what you think will happen. 20

problem: A problem is something that causes difficulties, or that makes you worry. 33

recycle: If you recycle things that have already been used, such as bottles or sheets of paper, you process them so that they can be used again. 57

reuse: When you reuse something, you use it again instead of throwing it away. 49

senses: Your senses are your physical ability to see, smell, hear, touch and taste. 24

solution: A solution is a way of dealing with a problem. 33

waste: Waste is something we do not use or need. 49

Acknowledgements

The publishers gratefully acknowledge the permission granted to reproduce copyright material in this book. Every effort has been made to trace copyright holders and to obtain their permission for the use of copyright material. The publishers will gladly receive any information enabling them to rectify any error or omission at the first opportunity. The publishers would like to thank the following for permission to reproduce copyright material:

Cover and title page Riccardo Mayer/Shutterstock, p.1 Monkey Business Images/Shutterstock, p.2 DisobeyArt/Shutterstock, p.2 goodluz/Shutterstock, p.2 StockImageFactory.com, p.2 takayuki/Shutterstock, p.3 iris828/Shutterstock, p.3 iris828/Shutterstock, p.3 BNP Design Studio/Shutterstock, p.7 Colorfuel Studio/Shutterstock, p.9 Studio Romantic, p.10 Monkey Business Images/Shutterstock, p.10 fizkes/Shutterstock, p.10 Lopolo/Shutterstock, p.10 kudla/Shutterstock, p.10 cdrin/Shutterstock, p.12 vuttichai chaiya/Shutterstock, p.14 Yuriy Golub/Shutterstock, p.15 KanKhem/Shutterstock, p.16 Volurol/Shutterstock, p.16 Wazzkii/Shutterstock, p.16 Urbanscape/Shutterstock, p.17 Rosemarie Gearhart/Shutterstock, p.18 Fotokostic/Shutterstock, p.18 ibragimova/Shutterstock, p.18 Toey Toey/Shutterstock, p.18 Prostock-studio/Shutterstock, p.18 JOKE_PHATRAPONG/Shutterstock, p.18 Hung Chung Chih/Shutterstock, p.19 Rock and Wasp/Shutterstock, p.19 ArtStudioHouse/Shutterstock, p.20 Idol Design/Shutterstock, p.24 passengerz/Shutterstock, p.24 VanoVasaio/Shutterstock, p.24 Nataly Studio/Shutterstock, p.24 Elena_E/Shutterstock, p.24 Peter Zijlstra/Shutterstock, p.24 kevin brine/Shutterstock, p.25 etorres/Shutterstock, p.25 Yeti studio/Shutterstock, p.25 HandmadePictures/Shutterstock, p.25 akepong srichaichana/Shutterstock, p.25 SAKORNJ/Shutterstock, p.25 Stephen R. Johnson / Alamy Stock Photo, p.25 asiandelight/Shutterstock, p.25 unguryanu/Shutterstock, p.26 inacio pires/Shutterstock, p.26 Olena Kibryk/Shutterstock, p.26 Wipat Boonkaew/Shutterstock, p.26 Niny2405/Shutterstock, p.26 Daisy Liang/Shutterstock, p.26 Sixsmith/Shutterstock, p.26 Maliutina Anna/Shutterstock, p.26 Anne Greenwood/Shutterstock, p.26 barmalini/Shutterstock, p.26 yuris/Shutterstock, p.27 asharkyu/Shutterstock, p.27 Dmitri Malyshev/Shutterstock, p.27 Tanya Yatsenko/Shutterstock, p.27 Aedka Studio/Shutterstock, p.28 Sorbis/Shutterstock, p.28 Pavel L Photo and Video/Shutterstock, p.28 Agarianna76/Shutterstock, p.28 Mita Stock Images/Shutterstock, p.28 BE_KUSHAGRA/Shutterstock, p.28 Rawpixel.com/Shutterstock, p.29 Arina P Habich/Shutterstock, p.29 Tada Images/Shutterstock, p.29 Goncharov_Artem/Shutterstock, p.29 SeventyFour/Shutterstock, p.29 DenysHolovatiuk/Shutterstock, p.32 matimix/Shutterstock, p.32 paulaphoto/Shutterstock, p.32 shutting/Shutterstock, p.32 MIA Studio/Shutterstock, p.32 Drazen Zigic/Shutterstock, p.32 Prostock-studio/Shutterstock, p.33 Nowaczyk/Shutterstock, p.34 Brastock/Shutterstock, p.34 leoks/Shutterstock, p.34 Vedaant Sethia/Shutterstock, p.34 Marek Poplawski/Shutterstock, p.34 i am adventure/Shutterstock, p.34 WhiteYura/Shutterstock, p.34 Santhosh Varghese/Shutterstock, p.34 mbrand85/Shutterstock, p.36 FabrikaSimf/Shutterstock, p.37 Talukdar David/Shutterstock, p.37 Kdonmuang/Shutterstock, p.37 DenisProduction.com/Shutterstock, p.38 OlegD/Shutterstock, p.38 Himanshu Saraf/Shutterstock, p.38 alexmisu/Shutterstock, p.38 Stefan Milivojevic/Shutterstock, p.38 KMLynch/Shutterstock, p.38 HM Shahidul Islam/Shutterstock, p.39 LEON_PHOTOGRAPHY/Shutterstock, p.39 Irondaru/Shutterstock, p.39 Stanislaw Mikulski/Shutterstock, p.39 Cathy Withers-Clarke/Shutterstock, p.40 mauritius images GmbH / Alamy Stock Photo, p.40 Evgeniy pavlovski/Shutterstock, p.40 Ljupco Smokovski/Shutterstock, p.40 OlegD/Shutterstock, p.40 Ruth Black/Shutterstock, p.40 Maridav/Shutterstock, p.40 Byron Ortiz/Sutterstock, p.41 afaf.asf/Shutterstock, p.42 Frezi Gate/Shutterstock, p.42 Siwakorn1933/Shutterstock, p.42 Nik Merkulov/Shutterstock, p.42 marla dawn studio/Shutterstock, p.42 SB Freelancer/Shutterstock, p.42 studiovin/Shutterstock, p.44 Repina Valeriya/Shutterstock, p.44 Lukas_Vejrik/Shutterstock, p.44 Gray Moeller/Shutterstock, p.46 IanRedding/Shutterstock, p.46 Romolo Tavani/Shutterstock, p.46 Vallarista/Shutterstock, p.46 R_Tee/Shutterstock, p.47 Eakrin Rasadonyindee/Shutterstock, p.47 RosnaniMusa/Shutterstock, p.47 PhotoAlto sas / Alamy Stock Photo, p.47 Igisheva Maria/Shutterstock, p.47 Jaromir Chalabala/Shutterstock, p.47 VCoscaron / Alamy Stock Photo/Shutterstock, p.47 adrianadefernex/Shutterstock, p.47 rigsbyphoto/Shutterstock, p.47 Wanida_Sri/Shutterstock, p.47 Antikwar/Shutterstock, p.47 Joe MoJo/Shutterstock, p.47 Aluap Photography/Shutterstock, p.49 Elnur/Shutterstock, p.49 Josep Curto/Shutterstock, p.50 FabrikaSimf/Shutterstock, p.50 mayu85/Shutterstock, p.50 eryvall/Shutterstock, p.50 AtlasStudio, p.50 kibri_ho/Shutterstock, p.50 Peter Hermes Furian/Shutterstock, p.50 Roman Motizov/Shutterstock, p.50 kavring/Shutterstock, p.50 Octavian Lazar/Shutterstock, p.50 Martin Spurny/Shutterstock, p.50 Tatiana Popova/Shutterstock, p.50 catinsyrup/Shutterstock, p.50 HANUMAN_168/Shutterstock, p.50 Runrun2/Shutterstock, p.50 DONOT6_STUDIO/Shutterstcok, p.50 Rae Alexander/Shutterstock, p.53 Gargonia/Shutterstock, p.53 Rawpixel.com/Shutterstock, p.53 Robert Kneschke/Shutterstock, p.53 yalayama/Shutterstock, p.53 wavebreakmedia/Shutterstock, p.53 Maples Images/Shutterstock, p.54 Four Oaks/Shutterstock, p.54 Paul Vinten/Shutterstock, p.54 Tom Reichner/Shutterstock, p.54 Wright Out There/Shutterstock, p.54 cynb/Shutterstock, p.54 Quinn Kampschroer/Shutterstock, p.54 Vladimir Melnik/Shutterstock, p.55 Tavarius/Shutterstock, p.55 Dontree_M/Shutterstock, p.55 SunisaStock/Shutterstock, p.55 Quang Ho/Shutterstock, p.55 Widhibek/Shutterstock, p.55 Mr.Emre.B/Shutterstock, p.57 wavebreakmedia/Shutterstock, p.58 Guas/Shutterstock, p.60 Inked Pixels/Shutterstock, p.60 Andrea Cupolillo/Shutterstock, p.60 NOVODIASTOCK/Shutterstock, p.60 Gerry Bishop/Shutterstock, p.60 Nature Peaceful/Shutterstock, p.60 Kristine Rad/Shutterstock, p.62 Carbonero Stock/Shutterstock, p.63 Zzzenia/Shutterstock, p.63 Elena Hramova/Shutterstock, p.63 szefei/Shutterstock, p.63 Christine8/Shutterstock, p.64 Zzzenia/Shutterstock, p.65 wavebreakmedia/Shutterstock, p.66 stas11/Shutterstock, p.66 TimeImage Production/Shutterstock, p.66 maxim ibragimov/Shutterstock, p.67 Cobalt/AdobeStock, p.67 Daboost/Shutterstock, p.67 Zaharah Binti Aris/Shutterstock, p.67 PRILL/Shutterstock, p.67 ThalesAntonio/Shutterstock, p.67 FotoDuets/Shutterstock, p.68 Florent Lacroute/Shutterstock, p.68 Radiokafka/Shutterstock, p.69 Simple Line/Shutterstock, p.69 galimovma79/Shutterstock, p.69 Singleline/Shutterstock, p.69 Dilyaab/Shutterstock, p.69 Sarah2/Shutterstock, p.69 RNko7/Shutterstock, p.70 BNP Design Studio/Shutterstock, p.71 Pressmaster/Shutterstock, p.72 SUKJAI PHOTO/Shutterstock, p.72 Ben Gingell/Shutterstock, p.72 ViDI Studio/Shutterstock, p.72 HuanPhoto/Shutterstock, p.73 2j architecture/Shutterstock, p.73 Anna_Kuzmina/Shutterstock, p.73 aleksandr paraev/Shutterstock, p.73 VGstockstudio/Shutterstock, p.73 wavebreakmedia/Shutterstock, p.73 1485923375/Shutterstock, p.74 Kuznetsov Dmitriy/Shutterstock, p.75 BNP Design Studio/Shutterstock, p.77 Brastock/Shutterstock, p.77 Anatoliy Karlyuk/Shutterstock, p.77 yalayama/Shutterstock, p.78 Littlekidmoment/Shutterstock, p.79 Ground Picture/Shutterstock, p.79 fizkes/Shutterstock, p.79 pamela4578/123rf.